First World War
and Army of Occupation
War Diary
France, Belgium and Germany

59 DIVISION
Divisional Troops
Royal Army Service Corps
Divisional Train (513,514,515,516, Companies A.S.C.)
1 January 1916 - 30 June 1916

WO95/3019/3

The Naval & Military Press Ltd
www.nmarchive.com
Published in association with The National Archives

Published by

The Naval & Military Press Ltd

Unit 10 Ridgewood Industrial Park,

Uckfield, East Sussex,

TN22 5QE England

Tel: +44 (0) 1825 749494

www.naval-military-press.com

www.nmarchive.com

This diary has been reprinted in facsimile from the original. Any imperfections are inevitably reproduced and the quality may fall short of modern type and cartographic standards.

© Crown Copyright

Images reproduced by permission of The National Archives, London, England, 2015.

Contents

Document type	Place/Title	Date From	Date To
Heading	WO95/3019/3 Divisional Train (513,514,515,516 Companies A.S.C)		
Heading	War Diary Of O.C. A.S.C 59th (N. Mid) Div Train From 1st To 31st January 1916		
War Diary	Stalbans	01/01/1916	25/01/1916
War Diary	War Diary Of O C Hd Qr Coy 59th (N Mid) Div Train From 1st To 31st January 1916 Vol I		
War Diary	Boxmoor	01/01/1916	29/01/1916
Heading	War Diary Of O C No.2 Coy 59th (N Mid) Div Train From 1st To 31st January 1916 Vol I		
War Diary	St Albans	01/01/1916	25/01/1916
War Diary	Boxmoor	29/01/1916	29/01/1916
War Diary	St Albans	01/01/1916	31/01/1916
Heading	No.3 Co A S C 59th (N.M) Div War Diary Period 1st To 31st January 1916		
War Diary	Sopwell House St Albans	01/01/1916	28/01/1916
Heading	War Diary Of O C No Company A S C 59th (N.M) Division Walford From Jany 1st To Jany 31st 1916		
War Diary	Watford	04/01/1916	25/01/1916
Heading	War Diary Of O C No 573 Coy A S C 59th (N Mid) Div From 1st To 29th Feby 1916 Vol II		
War Diary	Boxmoor	01/02/1916	29/02/1916
Heading	War Diary Of No 515 Company Army Service Corps 59th (N.M) Division From 010216 To 290216		
War Diary	Boxmoor	01/02/1916	01/02/1916
War Diary	St Albans	01/02/1916	16/02/1916
War Diary	Watford	17/02/1916	29/02/1916
Heading	War Diary Of No 516 Coy A S C 59 (NM) Div From February 1st 1916 To February 29th 1916 Vol II		
War Diary	Watford	02/02/1916	16/02/1916
War Diary	St Albans	17/02/1916	29/02/1916
Heading	War Diary Of O.C. A.S.C. 59th (N Mid) Divisional Train From Feb 1st 1916 To Feb 29th 1916 Vol 2		
War Diary	St Albans	02/02/1916	29/02/1916
War Diary	War Diary Vol II Of O.C 514th Coy A.S.C. 59th N.M Division From Feb 1916 To 1916 Jun		
War Diary	Sopwell House St Albans	05/02/1916	29/02/1916
War Diary	Boxmoor	01/02/1916	01/02/1916
War Diary	St Albans	01/02/1916	16/02/1916
War Diary	Watford	17/02/1916	25/04/1916
War Diary	Kingstown Reland	25/04/1916	27/04/1916
War Diary	Kilmainhani Hospital	28/04/1916	16/05/1916
War Diary	Balls Bridge Dublin	17/05/1916	27/05/1916
War Diary	Old Barracks Fermoy	28/05/1916	30/06/1916

W095/30191/3
Dismissal Train (513, 514, 515, 516
Companies A, S, C)

Confidential .   Vol I .

HEADQUARTERS
A.S.C.
No..........
Date..........
59th (N.M.) DIVISION.

30

War Diary.
of
O.C. A.S.C. 59th (2 Mid) Div Train.
from.
1st to 31st January 1916.

Confidential

WAR DIARY or INTELLIGENCE SUMMARY

Army Form C. 2118.

59th (N.M.) DIVISION.

Place	Date	Hour	Summary of Events and Information	Remarks and references to Appendices
ST ALBANS.	1.1.16		LT.T.M. HAZLERIGG took over command of No.3 COY from CAPT. C.H. CLARK who was transferred to T.F. Reserve.	
"	4.1.16		I took over command of the train, on my return from FRANCE, from CAPT A.T. WILLIAMS.	2.S.R.
"	5.1.16		I proceeded to ALDERSHOT for the purpose of attending a course for senior Officers. CAPT. A.T. WILLIAMS took over command of the train.	2.S.R.
"	15.1.16		23 Drivers reported from 3rd Line & were posted to Coys of the train.	2.S.R.
"	19.1.16		Reported for duty on return from ALDERSHOT, CAPT A.T. WILLIAMS relinquished Command and 2nd LT T.G. SIMMONS & 2nd LT H. WOOD reported for duty from 3rd Line, the former was posted to No.4 Coy & the latter to HdQrs Coy.	2.S.R.
"	24.1.16			2.S.R.
"	25.1.16		CAPT & ADJ S.R. THORNBERY & LT A.N. PEACH left for ALDERSHOT for the purpose of attending a course in Transport & Supply duties. LT. J.K. BROWN appointed Acting Adjutant. All Transport & Supply duties have been carried out by the train during the month & all 1st line Transport has been inspected by me.	2.S.R.

E.G. Ramsay.
Lieut. Colonel.
Commdg. A.S.C. 59th (N.M.) Divn.

Confidential

(31)

War Diary

of

O.C., Hd Qr Coy. 59th (N.Mid.) Divl Train

from 1st to 31st January, 1916.

(Vol. I.)

WAR DIARY
INTELLIGENCE SUMMARY
(Erase heading not required.)

Army Form C. 2118

Instructions regarding War Diaries and Intelligence Summaries are contained in F.S. Regs., Part II. and the Staff Manual respectively. Title Pages will be prepared in manuscript.

Place	Date	Hour	Summary of Events and Information	Remarks and references to Appendices
BOXMOOR	1/1/16		HQuarters at Felden Bosmoor Herts.	
"	4/1/16		18 N.C.O.s and men on Stretcher - at markyate D.C.M. on No. 625.87. H. Evans at 2 p.m.	
"	21/1/16		3A + Servym 195th Field Amb Exercise of same	
"	23/1/16		Inspection of Horses by the A.D.V.S.	
"	25/1/16		2 Lieut H. Morel reports for duty from 3rd Line	
"	29/1/16		Transferred Headquarters by m.t. to Captain A.J. Williams R.E.	

(P.T.O.)

Army Form C. 2118.

WAR DIARY
INTELLIGENCE SUMMARY.
(Erase heading not required.)

Instructions regarding War Diaries and Intelligence Summaries are contained in F. S. Regs., Part II. and the Staff Manual respectively. Title pages will be prepared in manuscript.

Place	Date	Hour	Summary of Events and Information	Remarks and references to Appendices
BOXMOOR	29/1/16		Took over Command of Hd Qrs Coy. A.S.C. from Major R.J. Green A.P. Williams Capt. A.S.C. (T.F.)	

Confidential

WAR DIARY
— of —
O.C., No. 2 Coy, 59th (N.Mid) Div'l Train

from 1st to 31st January, 1916.

(Vol. I.)

Army Form C. 2118.

WAR DIARY
~~INTELLIGENCE SUMMARY~~
(Erase heading not required.)

Instructions regarding War Diaries and Intelligence Summaries are contained in F. S. Regs, Part II. and the Staff Manual respectively. Title pages will be prepared in manuscript.

Place	Date	Hour	Summary of Events and Information	Remarks and references to Appendices
ST. ALBANS	1/1/16		In Quarters at ST ALBANS	ASC
"	5/1/16 to 19/1/16		Took over temporary command of 59th (N.Mid) Div. Train during absence on duty of Lt-Col. L.G. Reading. Lieut A.N. Peel assumed temporary command of No. 2 Coy.	ASC
"	25/1/16		Lieut A.N. Peel proceeds to ALDERSHOT for Course of Instruction in A.S.C. Duties.	ASC
BOXMOOR	29/1/16		Took over command of Hd Qr Coy 59th (N.Mid) Div. Train at BOXMOOR. 2/Lieut. R.D. Beet took over temporary command of No. 2 Coy.	ASC
ST. ALBANS	1/1/16 to 31/1/16		General Routine Duties	ASC

M. Williams Capt. A.S.C.

No. 3 Co. A.S.C. 59th (N.M.) Div.

WAR DIARY.

Period 1st to 31st January 1916.

Army Form C. 2118.

WAR DIARY

~~INTELLIGENCE SUMMARY.~~

(Erase heading not required.)

Place	Date	Hour	Summary of Events and Information	Remarks and references to Appendices
SOPWELL HOUSE. ST. ALBANS.	1916 1 Jan'y.		LIEUT. T.M. HAZLERIGG took over command of No 3 Co. A.S.C. 59th (N.M.) Div. from CAPT. C.H. CLARK. Strength of Company being :- 4 Officers, 73 other ranks, plus 5 drivers for detachment to Headquarters of 176th Inf. Bde. Required to complete establishment :- 1 Officer, 2 Wheelers, 1 Saddler, 1 Motor Driver, 1 Private (Supply Detail), 1 Riding horse.	nutt.
"	5 Jan'y.		Received from 176th Inf. Bde. Hdqrs. Secret orders for instruction in event of Emergency Move.	nutt.
"	14 Jany		Pte JENNINGS discharged as Medically unfit for further service. (K. Regs. para 392 (xii)).	nutt.
"	17 Jan'y		Three horses R II taken on charge. Issued on each to No 2, No 4 Co. A.S.C. retaining one to complete establishment.	nutt.
"	28 Jany		Sergt. BULL discharged on being gazetted to 3/1 WARWICKSHIRE BATTY. R.G.A. 1 N.C.O. + 4 men detached to 176th Inf. Bde. Hdqrs.	nutt.

TMHazlerigg
Capt.
O.C. No. 3 Co., A.S.C.
59th (N.M.) Divn.

Confidential   516   Volume I

(34)

War Diary
of
O.C. No. 4 Company. A.S.C.
59th (N.M.) Division, Watford.

From Jany 1st to Jany 31st, 1916.

Army Form C. 2118.

WAR DIARY
or
INTELLIGENCE SUMMARY.
(Erase heading not required.) (7)

Instructions regarding War Diaries and Intelligence Summaries are contained in F. S. Regs., Part II. and the Staff Manual respectively. Title pages will be prepared in manuscript.

Hour, Date, Place	Summary of Events and Information	Remarks and references to Appendices
Jan 4th 16 WATFORD	14 men, 27 horses & 12 wagons attached from Hd Qr Coy for duty	17
Jan 5th 16 WATFORD	Mark I Wagons received. 8 new .13 transferred from this units. One of the rail travels were traced which rendered them unserviceable after they had been exposed to the wet. This was reported to D.A.D.O.S. with a view to having new ones issued before receiving	17
Jan 15th 16 WATFORD	7 men transferred from 3rd line to complete establishment.	17
Jan 25th 16 WATFORD	2/Lieut. G Simons transferred from 3rd line and taken on strength of the Coy.	17

Confidential

WAR DIARY

of

O.C. No 513 Coy, A.S.C., 59ᵗʰ (N.Mid) Div.

from 1ˢᵗ to 29ᵗʰ Feby, 1916.

(Vol. II.)

WAR DIARY
INTELLIGENCE SUMMARY.
(Erase heading not required.)

Army Form C. 2118.

× (513 Coy ASC)
5g H Q 2nd Div Train.

Instructions regarding War Diaries and Intelligence Summaries are contained in F.S. Regs., Part II. and the Staff Manual respectively. Title pages will be prepared in manuscript.

Place	Date	Hour	Summary of Events and Information	Remarks and references to Appendices
BOXMOOR	1/2/16		Qrs Quarters at FELDEN, BOXMOOR, HERTS.	ADS
	2/2/16		Div Route March	ADS
	9/2/16		Div Train Route March	ADS
	12/2/16		2 men reported from 3rd Line	ADS
	15/2/16		Capt. J.A. Sutton proceeds to ALDERSHOT for Course of Instruction Capt. F.J.C. Smith takes over duties of O. i/c Supplies, BOXMOOR, during absence on duty of Capt. Sutton	ADS
	17/2/16		Major A.T. Williams on 7 days leave	ADS
	20/2/16		Test Ration — Emergency Move, Table "B".	ADS
	1/2/16—29/2/16		General Routine Duties	ADS

H. Sillior
COMMDG. 513 COMPANY A.S.C.

Confidential.

War Diary

of

No. 515 Company Army Service Corps, 59th (N.M.) Division

From 1.2.16 to 29.2.16

L Green Capt
O/C No 515 Company, A.S.C.,
59th (N.M.) Division

WAR DIARY or INTELLIGENCE SUMMARY

Army Form C. 2118

5/15 Coy A.S.C.
59th (2nd Div) Div

Place	Date	Hour	Summary of Events and Information	Remarks and references to Appendices
BOXMOOR	1/1/16	9 a.m.	Inspected HdQrs Coy A.S.C. over to Capt Williams at FELDEN, BOXMOOR	DG
St ALBANS	1/1/16	10.20 a.m.	Took over No 2 Coy A.S.C. from Capt Williams at TOWER MOUNT, ST ALBANS	DG
"	2/1/16	11.45 a.m.	Inspection of Division by the G.O.C. at REDBOURNE	DG
"	9/1/16	12.15 p.m.	Inspection of the Divisional Train at REDMOND by the G.O.C	DG
"	16/1/16	10.0 p.m.	Moved to CASSIOBRIDGE, WATFORD	DG
WATFORD	17/1/16		In quarters at CASSIOBRIDGE WATFORD	
"	29/1/16	10.40 a.m.	Received orders to move on Emergency Railway Entrainment Scheme (Trial B) (Practising)	DG
"	29/1/16	10.45 a.m.	Received orders that the Brigade would move on Emergency Railway entrainment scheme. Commenced to issue Iron and Provisions return at 11.15 A.M.	DG
"	29/1/16	4.15 p.m.	Moved out of quarters to Entrain being inspected by the BDE COMdR at 5.30 p.m. at WATFORD JUNCTION and ordered to return to BILLETS	DG

Abrey Capt - 5/15 Coy A.S.C.

CONFIDENTIAL
WAR DIARY
OF
No 516 COY A.S.C.
59ᵗʰ (N.M) DIV.

FROM FEBRUARY 1ˢᵗ 1916 TO FEBRUARY 29ᵗʰ 1916

(VOL 18)

Army Form C. 2118.

WAR DIARY
or
INTELLIGENCE SUMMARY.
(Erase heading not required.)

516 Coy ASC
59-(NM) Div (8)

Hour, Date, Place	Summary of Events and Information	Remarks and references to Appendices
February 2nd /16 WATFORD	The Coy was inspected on the march by LIEUT. GEN. SIR A.E. CODRINGTON, K.C.V.O, C.B. Comdg 3rd Army.	17
February 14-15/16 WATFORD	The Coy was redesignated 516 Coy ASC 59-(NM) DIV.	17
February 16th/16 WATFORD.	The Company proceeded to ST ALBANS by road and took over the quarters of 515 Coy ASC 59th (NM)X-T	17
February 17th/16 ST ALBANS	CSM BISHOP died whilst on leave	17
Feby 24th/16 ST ALBANS	C.S.M. HADFIEL transferred to this Company.	17
February 29th/16 ST ALBANS.	TEST PRACTICE of EMERGENCY ENTRAINMENT SCHEME. Owing to many of the wagons being out on a wood convoy at WATFORD and the 177th INF. BDE to which this Company is now attached being at HARPENDEN 9 were unable to load the wagons with rations and dispatch them in time for them to report to their respective troops units before their time to march.	17

Chris Hadfield
Capt

Confidential

War Diary.
of
O.C. A.S.C. 59th (2 Irish) Divisional Train.

from Feb 1st 1916 to Feb 29th 1916.

VOL. 2.

Army Form C. 2118.

WAR DIARY
or
INTELLIGENCE SUMMARY.
(Erase heading not required.)

VOL. 2.
59th 2 Mid Div Train.
St Albans.

Place	Date	Hour	Summary of Events and Information	Remarks and references to Appendices
ST. ALBANS	2.2.16		Divisional Punch 9 inspection by Lt. Gen. Sir A.E. Codrington, K.C.V.O., C.B., Deputy 4B.9/1/gC wagons were curled in for service, funnelled with the Harness	
"	9.2.16		Capt. R.J. Green took over command of No 2 Coy.	LSA.
"	12.2.16		Capt & Adj S.R. Thornbery resumed duty as Adjutant on return from Aldershot. Train exercise in March discipline, conforming as far as possible with tactical arrangements. Eight drivers reported for duty to the train & were posted to Coys.	LSA.
"	15.2.16		Train Coys were reinspected H.R. Coy (313) No 2 (515), No 3 (514), No 4 (376).	LSA.
"	16.2.16		Capt J.A. Sutton & Lt A.C. Brown left their respective stations for a course at Aldershot. 515 Coy left St Albans for Watford & 516 Coy left Watford for St Albans.	LSA.
"	17.2.16		2nd Lt Plaistowe & 14 men left Watford for Bishops Stortford for duty with one the Supply depot from 61st S.Mid.Div. 2 drivers & horses & 2 wagons from 514 Coy, left for Bishops Stortford, for help.	LSA.
"	"		C.S. Major Bishop J.T. No 516 Coy proceed away at his home & is retired off the strength of the Coy.	
"	22.2.16		Major Jones H.W. S.S.O. left for Aldershot on duty.	LSA.
"	24.2.16		15 Horses arrived & were allotted to H.Q & 3. Coy. Boxmore.	LSA.
"	29.2.16		Received secret orders to put into force Table 13 (Practice).	LSA.

P.G. Manning
Lieut. Colonel,
Commdg. A.S.C. 59th (N.M.) Divn.

Confidential

War Diary Vol II
of
O.C. 514th Coy A.S.C
59th N.M. Division

from Feb 1st 1916 to Feb 29th 1916

1916 FEB — 14th JUN

Army Form C. 2118.

WAR DIARY

~~INTELLIGENCE SUMMARY.~~

(Erase heading not required.)

VOL. 1.

514 Coy A.S.C.
59th (2nd N. Midl) Divn

Instructions regarding War Diaries and Intelligence Summaries are contained in F. S. Regs., Part II. and the Staff Manual respectively. Title pages will be prepared in manuscript.

Place	Date 1916	Hour	Summary of Events and Information	Remarks and references to Appendices
SOPWELL HOUSE. ST ALBANS.	February 5th		Pte RICE. B. transferred from 2/5 Bathn. Lincs. Regt. + taken on strength of Company.	That
	7th		36 N.C.O's and men transferred from the Transport Section 2/3rd N.M. FIELD AMBULANCE. R.A.M.C. 15 N°3 Co. A.S.C. 59th (N.M.) Div. and attached to 2/3rd N.M. FIELD AMBULANCE. R.A.M.C.	That
	12th		Official designation of Company changed to 514 Coy. A.S.C.	
			L/Sgt. WALKER transferred from N° 513 Coy to N° 514 Coy. and taken on strength.	That
	14th		Drivers KILBY. HUGHES & GRIMLEY transferred from N.M. Div. Train (3rd Line) and taken on strength. One horse (R.I. N° 3765) transferred to Rough Riding School, LUTON.	That
	17th		One Sergeant, 1 L/Cpl, 1 Driver proceeded to BISHOPS STORTFORD on detached duty, with 2 G.S. Wagons, 4 H.D. horses.	That
	18th		Sergt. CRANE returned from detached duty at BISHOPS STORTFORD.	That
	23rd		War Establishment Part VIII in force. Div. Order 332.	That
	29th		Dr ATKINS proceeded to BISHOPS STORTFORD by Road route with one H.D. horse.	That
		10.30 A.M.	Received secret order turning into force Emergency Scheme, Table B. Test practice only. N°1 Train leaving 6 p.m. units to parade at their Headquarters ready to move but not to move. Second order received cancelling orders. On return of programme sent by units to At time of receipt of order 19 wagons on convoy duty. Paraded Headquarters of Company at 3 p.m. Supply Depot, last leaving SOPWELL at 1.40 p.m.	

T. M. Hargreaves
Capt.
O.C. No. 514 Co., A.S.C.
59th (N.M.) Divn.

ST. ALBANS

WAR DIARY
or
INTELLIGENCE SUMMARY
(Erase heading not required.)

Army Form C. 2118

Staff Coy

Place	Date	Hour	Summary of Events and Information	Remarks and references to Appendices
BOXMOOR	1/7/16	9 am	Inspected HdQrs Cy. A.S.C. over to Capt William at FELDEN. BOXMOOR	CL
St ALBANS	1/7/16	10.30 am	Took over No 2 Cy. A.S.C. from Capt. William at ROSEMOUNT St ALBANS	CL
"	2/7/16	11.45 am	Inspection of Division by the G.O.C. at REDBOURNE.	CL
"	9/7/16	12-15 pm	Inspection of the Ammunition Train at BEDMOND by the G.O.C.	CL
"	16/7/16	10.0 am	Moved to CASSIOBRIDGE. WATFORD.	CL
WATFORD	17/7/16		In quarters at CASSIOBRIDGE WATFORD.	CL
"	29/7/16	10.40 am	Received orders to move on Emergency Railway Entrainment scheme (Table B) (Practising)	CL
"	29/7/16	10.45 am	Received orders that the Brigade would not be entraining. Companies to feed horses and prisoners. Horses at 11.15 A.M.	CL
"	29/7/16	7.15 pm	Moved out of quarters to Entrain. being inspected by the B.O.C. Com Dr at 8.30 a.m. at WATFORD JUNCTION and ordered to return to BILLETS	CL

Army Form C. 2118

WAR DIARY
or
INTELLIGENCE SUMMARY
(Erase heading not required.)

Instructions regarding War Diaries and Intelligence Summaries are contained in F. S. Regs., Part II. and the Staff Manual respectively. Title Pages will be prepared in manuscript.

Place	Date	Hour	Summary of Events and Information	Remarks and references to Appendices
WATFORD	1/12		In quarters at CASSIO BRIDGE, WATFORD.	
"	9/12	2 p.m.	Inspection of all Horses by Col Stroh DADR. No 2 Circle.	
"	17/12	11 a.m.	Col Friel Inspector of Reserves visited the Station.	
"	22/12	10 a.m.	Exercises in Repelling Raiders - troops into Castle Green.	
"	23/12	11.15 a.m.	Depôt inspected by Major Stokes DAQMG 59th Division	

Asbury Capt.
O/C 515 Coy A.S.C. 59th (N.M.) Div.

WAR DIARY
or
INTELLIGENCE SUMMARY
(Erase heading not required.)

Army Form C. 2118

Place	Date	Hour	Summary of Events and Information	Remarks and references to Appendices
WATFORD	1/4/16		In quarters at Cassio Bridge, Watford, Herts.	
"	24/4/16	7.30 p.m.	Ordered to move at short notice from Divn HQrs	
"	"	8.30 p.m.	Definite orders from Divl HQrs to move, train time being notified. All wagon allotted to units of Bde sent out complete	
"	25/4/16	4.0 a.m.	The Coy HQrs with the Bde HQrs 178th Regt. Watford Junction	
KINGSTOWN IRELAND	25/4/16	10.30 p.m.	Arrived and disembarked	
"	26/4/16	9.30 a.m.	Ordered to Dublin Castle to give assistance to 176 & 178 Bde owing to lack of A.S.C. horsed transport - not being available to do both supplies and transport - for these two Bdes. Had to leave all baggage & equipment behind - the emergency	
"	2/5/16	9.30 a.m.	Ordered to move with remnants of 59th move to DUBLIN	
"	27/4/16		within 2 miles of Kilmainham Hospital, Dublin. the convoy was attacked and held up for some hours by the rebel snipers	
"	"	8.0 p.m.	arrived in Kilmainham Park without casualties	

Army Form C. 2118

WAR DIARY
or
INTELLIGENCE SUMMARY
(Erase heading not required.)

Instructions regarding War Diaries and Intelligence Summaries are contained in F.S. Regs., Part II. and the Staff Manual respectively. Title Pages will be prepared in manuscript.

Place	Date	Hour	Summary of Events and Information	Remarks and references to Appendices
KILMAINHAM HOSPITAL	28/4/16		In quarters.	
"	29/4/16	12 noon	Lieut. R.O. Bear wounded with the Transport sent to hospital the 176th Bn.	
"	30/4/16		In quarters at Royal Kilmainham Hospital Dublin. Green Cup- Me. 2	

Army Form C. 2118

Place	Date	Hour	Summary of Events and Information	Remarks and references to Appendices
KILMAINHAM HOSPITAL	3/16		In quarters at the Stables, Kilmainham Hospital.	
"	16/5/16	4.0 p.m	Moved his quarters at — Balls Bridge, Dublin on being Transferred to the 177th Brigade.	
BALLS BRIDGE DUBLIN	17/16		In quarters	
"	27/5/16	12 noon	Entrained for Fermoy. Co. Cork.	
OLD BARRACKS FERMOY.	28/5/16		In quarters	
"	31/5/16		In quarters at the Old Barracks.	

WAR DIARY
or
INTELLIGENCE SUMMARY
(Erase heading not required.)

Army Form C. 2118

1916

Place	Date	Hour	Summary of Events and Information	Remarks and references to Appendices
OLD BARRACKS FERMOY	1/2/16		No parades —	A/1
"	2/2/16		A special fortnight day training programme commenced —	A/2
"	13/2/16		Two days rest of inspection by the C.O. —	A/3
"	31/2/16		No parades at the OLD BARRACKS, FERMOY. —	A/4

Green Cape —
O.C. No 2 Coy. A.S.C.
59TH (N.M.) DN.

Army Form C. 2118

WAR DIARY
or
INTELLIGENCE SUMMARY
(Erase heading not required.)

Place	Date	Hour	Summary of Events and Information	Remarks and references to Appendices
OLD BARRACKS FERMOY	1/6/16		In quarters –	GS
"	17/6/16		sixteen N.C.O and men arrived from 3rd line unit –	GS
"	23/6/16		two drivers sent back to 8th Provisional Bde. A.S.C. SOUTHMINSTER	GS
"	30/6/16		In quarters at the OLD BARRACKS	GS

H Green Capt –

O.C. No 2 COY. A.S.C.
59TH (N.M.) DIV.

www.ingramcontent.com/pod-product-compliance
Lightning Source LLC
Chambersburg PA
CBHW081503160426
43193CB00014B/2583